Cowslip Corner

Published August 2004

© Copyright: Marylyn Wheat 2004

Printed by: ProPrint
Riverside Cottage
Great North Road
Stibbington
Peterborough
PE8 6LR

ISBN: 1-904985-11-4

For my family who adore animals - and all the children who may never see any of these animals in their natural habitat.

Also my thanks to 'Jude' who typed most of these pages during her lunch break in the office.

CONTENTS

Springtime
- Chapter 1 7
- Chapter 2 12
- Chapter 3 18

Late Spring
- Chapter 1 26
- Chapter 2 32
- Chapter 3 36
- Chapter 4 40

Summer
- Chapter 1 49
- Chapter 2 55
- Chapter 3 59
- Chapter 4 65

Late Summer
- Chapter 1 69
- Chapter 2 72
- Chapter 3 76
- Chapter 4 81

Springtime

Chapter One

Harry Hedgehog yawned and blinked both his eyes. He'd been fast asleep for a long while, in fact three or four months. He was rather late in waking; spring had already arrived. Lots of flowers were nodding their heads in the breeze and the birds were sitting high up in the tree tops. Harry yawned again, stretched and started to shuffle out of his bed which was in a pile of leaves in an old rabbit hole filled with dried leaves and twigs, and very cosy through the cold winter months.

Harry looked about him. The sun was starting to sink in the west looking like a big red ball so Harry realised that it was late afternoon. Suddenly he remembered, he had promised to meet his friends. He did hope they would be there in the place that they had planned to meet. They had all thought it a very good idea to keep in touch and find out if each of them were happy after the long, gloomy, cold months. It was agreed that early in the spring would be a good time to gather and have a little chat. During the hot summer there was absolutely no time for this as all the animals were kept busy eating and looking after their families. Once again Harry yawned and smelled the air. How lovely and fresh it was. There had been rain because the ground around him was very wet, but that was just what Harry needed to find big fat slugs and insects to fill his tummy up again. Harry plodded through the long wet grass and thick stemmed dandelions, pausing every now and again to look around him and enjoy the beautiful spring afternoon.

After about half an hour Harry was getting quite near the spot where he was to meet all his friends. He knew this because he had seen some 'munchies' in the distance chewing the grass. (Munchies was the name that Harry had for cows.) Suddenly, he was there, in Cowslip Corner. The people had named it because in the early summer the meadow was covered in cowslips just like a large yellow carpet. On one side of the meadow was woodland, on the other two sides there were tall hedges which were covered in blackberries in late summer. How the blackbirds loved to pick those berries, and the people, would come with baskets to pick all the juicy fruit. Harry didn't particularly care for them, which was good, because there was no way that Harry could reach them anyhow. On the far side of the meadow ran a small river, not deep, but with clear blue water in which little silver fish darted to and fro. Kenny Kingfisher would sit on a branch of the large willow tree that grew close to the river and when he spotted a little silver fish sparkling in the sunshine, he would dart down and whisk the little fish up in his beak. He really didn't have to work hard at all to find his breakfast. The small frogs that lived in the river would hide in mud and tall rushes that grew by the water; they would only come out in the evening to play their games. There were lots and lots of frogs. Their families grew larger every year, so now and again the young frogs would have to hop away and find new homes for themselves and their children. They joined up in groups and hopped through the meadow, often heading towards the busy road. This was very dangerous for them because they didn't know about motor cars and sometimes kind people would see one of them on the road and pick him up and gently place him on the grass out of harm's way. Frogs and children have to be so very careful when they are crossing the road.

Harry was having another sniff at the nice fresh air when suddenly through the tall grass he saw them, some of his friends. There they were not very far away at all. He could see Willy Weasel, Bella and Billy Badger, Olive Otter and Red the squirrel who was hanging from a tree branch obviously eating some of last year's acorns and enjoying them very much.

'Hello there,' shouted Harry.
All his friend turned to him and shouted back, 'Hello Harry.'
Harry trundled over to them as fast as his little feet would take him. Then they all started chattering at once.

'Did you have a good sleep Harry?' asked Ollie. 'Did Ferdy Fox disturb you at all?'
Harry answered and told Ollie that he'd had a long, undisturbed rest and that he was looking forward to the summer months when he could travel all around the meadow and probably see some more of his friends. Billy and Bella Badger were quiet and Harry noticed this. 'What's the matter?' he asked. 'Are you both well?'
Billy turned to Harry and then he told him. 'We've had an awful time Harry, two or three times lately some men have come with dogs and tried to drive us out of our homes. We were very frightened.
Harry thought that was awful, which it was.
Billy then continued to speak, telling Harry and the rest of the animals what happened. They all listened to him and felt sad, but then Bill cheered up and said: 'The last time the men came with dogs they were followed by a boy and a girl who started to shout at them. For a while the men didn't bother and then the boy went up to one of the men and spoke to him. Soon the man turned round and called the other men and dogs to him. Then they left. Bella and I felt so happy that they had gone. We haven't seen them now for about three weeks, so maybe they

won't come again. I heard the girl call the boy Terry so Bella and I are going to call him King Terry. We haven't got a lion here to call King so that is who we'll have as our king.'

The other animals nodded their heads.
'What a good idea,' said Olive Otter. 'Anyone who takes care of us should be called a king, or I suppose if it's a lady then we'd call her Queen.'
'Oh, I think Terry called her Kim,' said Billy.

Right then, agreed all of the animals, that's what we'll call them, King Terry and Queen Kim.

'I like that,' said Harry. 'That makes us more important having a king and queen. We'll have to tell all the others about this.'
The animals felt happy about this idea, so they all cheered 'Hurrah for the King and Queen of Cowslip Corner.'

By now the sun had gone and the meadow started to get a little dark so the animals decided it was time to part. Off they went, all in different directions and promising to meet again at the end of summer.

Harry said goodbye to them. The only thing he could think of now was the lovely fat worms, slugs and other insects that he would find for his dinner. Then after that he would have a little nap until the sun came out again.

'Goodbye,' said Red the squirrel. And as he said it an acorn dropped out of his mouth. 'There'll be a young oak growing here this time next year Harry,' he said as Harry went off, nodding goodbye as he went.

Chapter Two

Drip-drip, drip-drip. Harry woke up with a start and then realised where he was. He'd eaten so much the night before that he'd just curled up in a ball by the hedge and gone to sleep. That was silly of me, he thought. Ferdy might have come along and annoyed me just for the fun of it. He wouldn't have liked to feel my spiky coat on his nose though, so probably he wouldn't. All the same it was silly of me not to have some cover over my body. With that Harry got up. The sky was grey. It had been raining and it was still raining, but just the job for Harry. He didn't mind at all. Looking for food was easier in the rain. It got so hot for him when the sun shone.

Suddenly he heard someone calling his name. Harry looked around and then saw who it was. 'Well, hello Freda, how are you?'

'I'm fine,' said Freda the field mouse. 'I'm just having a little exercise before Ferdy Fox comes out.'
'I shouldn't be too long,' said Harry, 'Ferdy will be out soon. No doubt he will go down to the farmyard and see what he can find there, but all the same I don't think you should be in the meadow when he comes running about. Did you know that we've got a king and queen now?'
Freda said she'd never heard of such a thing so Harry told her about the meeting he and his friends had had last night.

Freda squeaked with delight. Poor little thing, thought Harry, it must be hard for her when a large animal or person chases her, she's so tiny.

'Well bye bye,' said Freda. 'I'm going home now.' And with that she disappeared down a hole.

Well that was nice seeing Freda, thought Harry. I must look for some dinner now. Harry was lost in thought scraping a hole in some soft earth when, suddenly, there was such a noise. Harry looked up to where the noise was coming from. Then he saw Red who was scampering as fast as he could up to the top of a tree with a big black cat close behind him. Oh goodness, thought Harry, is that cat going to catch Red?

Harry watched. He couldn't do anything to help Red. The cat was getting closer when, all of a sudden, Red did a mighty jump and landed in another tree. 'Thank goodness,' said Harry. 'Red is safe now. I bet he was busy eating all those nuts and didn't even notice that cat prowling up to him.'

Harry stayed to see what the cat would do. It started to climb down the bark of the small tree, but it was easier going up than it was coming down because the rain had made the tree all wet and slippery. The cat kept sliding down and digging its claws into the tree bark to stop it falling. Just then a large crow flew overhead and cawed so loudly that it frightened the cat and the cat slipped and slipped until it fell to the ground. It sat there a while, licked itself, stood up and walked away. The animals didn't like cats chasing them, or dogs. They got very frightened. Harry trundled on and looked up to see the munchies still chewing away at the grass. Such a nice evening, thought Harry, so quiet now, and peaceful. I wonder where all my friends are?

In fact all Harry's friends were doing exactly as he was doing. They were busy looking for food and watching in case any large animals or people came into the meadow. After a while Harry started to feel tired. He'd been out for about four hours and soon it would be bedtime. The sun was going to shine again as it had stopped raining. Harry decided to walk to the riverside and find a bed there. As soon as he got nearer the river he heard voices. It wasn't his friends, the voices sounded so different. He stopped and looked and then he saw them. There were two people sitting by the side of the water, a girl and a boy. That must be King Terry and Queen Kim, thought Harry. I shall feel safe when I go to sleep if they are here. With that Harry curled into a ball and, as fast as lightning, he fell asleep.

Very soon the skies began to turn darker. The night was well on its way, and it seemed that everything in the meadow was becoming quieter, including the songs that the birds sang, and the gentle humming noise that the bees made. The silence was broken as the animals who were not already asleep heard people talking. It was the boy and girl sitting by the river, or the king and queen as Harry and his friends now called them. It was Kim who was speaking.

'Terry,' she said, 'I think we should be getting home now, Mummy and Daddy will be getting worried about us.'
'They know where we are,' replied Terry, splashing a stick in the water and making small ripples.
'But Terry, that doesn't matter,' said Kim. 'They will still be worried even so. We should be home before dark, you know that. If we don't do as we are asked and come home when we should Mummy and Daddy won't let us come out by ourselves anymore, and we both love to come out to this meadow. That was very brave of you the other day when you told that man he shouldn't be hunting the badgers. I didn't really think that he and the other man would leave, but you must have frightened them.'
'No more than they frightened the poor badgers,' said Terry. 'They knew I was right and there's a law against hunting badgers. It's so very cruel Kim. Two grown men and two dogs chasing a small animal out of its home, just to show off to their friends. They would have killed those badgers you know.'
'Oh don't say that,' said Kim. 'It's so terribly sad, how can they enjoy doing that?'
'Some people are just like that. They want to hunt and kill just for the sake of it. Not because they are hungry or they need food, just because they enjoy killing something weaker than themselves.'
'I'll never do that,' said Kim. 'I hope you never do.'
Terry answered, 'We should be friends with all the animals in the meadow. They are all our friends and too small to hurt us.

Once there was a very kind man called Francis and all the animals and the birds loved him. They would all come to him when he called. The birds and squirrels would sit on his shoulder and the rest of the animals would gather round his feet, even the tigers and the bears.'
'I don't believe it,' said Kim.
'It's true,' said Terry. 'Anyway we had better go now, it's really getting dark. You're right, Mummy and Daddy will be worried. I'll tell them we were busy talking about the animals and the time just slipped by.'

Terry and Kim made their way home by a small footpath that ran through the meadow and over a stile in the middle of the hedge. Kim cut herself on a sharp thorn.
'Oh just rub it,' said Terry. 'It will be alright. Don't complain or Mummy won't let you come again. She'll think you are still a little baby.'
'I'm not a baby,' said Kim and forgot all about her little cut.

They came to the road and looked both ways to see that no motor cars were coming before crossing over to the other side. In no time at all they were at their house. Mummy came out to meet them.

'Where have you been?' Mummy said. 'I was getting worried. It's dark now.'
'Sorry Mummy,' said Terry. 'We were sitting by the river and talking. The time just flew by, but here we are, both safe and sound and longing for a bath and a nice cosy bed.'
'All right then,' said Mummy, 'up those stairs you go and make sure you both get yourselves clean, and remember to brush your teeth before you get into bed. Daddy and I will come up

to say goodnight.'
Within an hour the two children were all tucked up in bed and fast asleep, just like Harry.

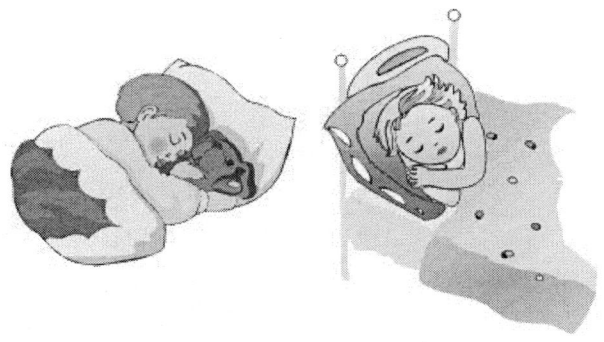

Chapter Three

Young Roger Rabbit had been hopping about for ages. He'd found quite enough to eat but he was so excited he wanted to tell Harry what had happened to him. Last autumn he had missed the meeting with Harry and his friends so he had been unable to tell his story. Roger lived in the meadow. In fact he lived in a lot of places. The tunnels to his home went right across the meadow, some under the hedge, some in the woodland and some in the field where the munchies stayed. He had an exciting life seeing lots of things that the animals who only lived in the meadow were unable to see. If he stood near one of his doorways in the summer when the sun shone, he would see the people coming out of buildings carrying bags. The buildings were where they kept their food. The mother of the little people would find a nice spot in the meadow, spread a cloth out and take the food out of the bags. Roger looked forward to these times because often the children wouldn't eat their lettuce, or the fat juicy tomatoes they would throw on the ground while Mummy wasn't looking. But Roger would notice and when all the people went home in the evening, Roger would come out of his house and enjoy a wonderful feast without even having to hunt for it. This was part of the reason why Roger got so fat last year. He was only a baby but he was fatter than all his brothers and sisters. But then, Roger was clever wasn't he? There was only one worry Roger had about these 'picnics', (this is what the people called them). He worried about all the bags the people left behind. Some of them you could see all the way through, not like the brown paper bags. These see-through bags were very dangerous and when the wind and rain came the see-through bags blew into the munchies' field. If a munchie was chewing a delicious clump of green grass she might not see the tiny screwed-up see-through bag and would accidentally swallow it with the grass. The bag would arrive in her tummy and get larger and larger until the munchie was not able to eat at all. If the farmer person saw the sick munchie he might say, 'I can't afford to keep you. You're giving me no milk to sell. You'll have to go away.' And the poor munchie would be taken away from all her friends, even though it wasn't her fault. Sometimes the big birds that lived on the river would also suffer because of these see-through bags. They would dip their beaks into the water and swallow the bag, all because the people didn't take their bags home with them and leave the meadow as pretty and clean as when they had found it. Roger was so busy thinking about these awful bags, when suddenly, someone pulled his little tail.

'Oh!' shouted Roger as he turned around. It's all right, I'm safe, he thought. It was just Harry that he'd woken up.

'Hello Roger,' said Harry. 'It's good to see you. I missed you yesterday when we all met.'

'I know,' said Roger, 'I was in the woods. I saw this awful looking thing in the grass. It was silver and it shone in the sunlight, but I didn't go near it. It must have been one of the people's things. How are you Harry?'

'I'm fine. I had a lovely, long winter sleep, all calm and safe.'

'You're very lucky,' said Roger. 'you must be careful when the man person from the cottage comes into the meadow, because he's not collecting dead leaves to put in his garden. He sets fire to them. I just happened to come out of one of my doorways last October, I noticed that the air in my tunnel smelt funny but it wasn't until I put my head outside that I found out why. The man person had set fire to some dead leaves by my door. And I burnt my whiskers! Luckily it was just my whiskers and they grew all nice and new again. It could have been my nose or my tail though and that wouldn't have grown back would it?'

'No,' said Harry. 'You were very lucky. I suppose I am too, although I'll have to look for a new bed this autumn.'

'Yes,' said Roger.

After Roger left, Harry decided that finding a new spot for a bed for the winter was his first task. He trundled around the meadow investigating all the holes and bushes that might give him shelter but he wasn't happy with any of them. Not far away from him was Freda Field Mouse. She was bobbing up and down by the hedge. Then Harry realised she was calling him.

'Harry, come here!' she was shouting. 'I bet you're looking for a new bed. I've been watching you. Am I right?'

'Yes you are,' said Harry and, following Freda, they ran along

by the side of the hedge.
Suddenly Freda stopped. 'There, look at that.'
Harry looked at where Freda was pointing and saw a small hole hidden at the bottom of a blackberry bush by the surrounding small branches and thorns.
'That looks just the job,' said Harry. 'No-one will see me there and the thorns will protect me should anything come too close to me and the wind and rain will not blow in because the bush is all around me. That's super Freda, thank you very much. It was very kind of you to help me.'
'That's all right Harry. You're my friend and that's what friends do – help each other.'

Harry was very, very pleased. Now that problem was out of the way he could enjoy the rest of the day till his bedtime with no worries at all.

It was night time. Most of the animals were curled up in their beds. Even Harry was because he couldn't wait to try out his new bed. The meadow was dark apart from a few rays of light cast by the moon shining, and through these shafts of light a family of bats were flying. This was the time they always came out to look for food. That was because the bats didn't have to see the things they were hunting for. They could hear them. The sound of a fly or mosquito or a moth, all of these the bats could hear. They are clever little animals. Just like field mice with wings. The bats lived in the old church in the village. Bats had lived there for many years and it was a perfect home for them. Even the sound of the church bells ringing didn't seem to bother them. Gradually the sky started to change colour. It was getting lighter. The family of bats all turned round and flew home to the church tower. In the woodland a pretty deer named Dainty was getting to her feet and shaking herself after her night's sleep. Dainty started to walk slowly and carefully along the woodland paths, always sniffing the air and listening to every sound. She was very nervous and frightened in case she met 'the people'. It had been a hard winter and Dainty was very hungry. Dainty walked slowly through the woodland, stopping to eat a juicy berry now and again. Gradually she came to the edge of the wood. Dainty smelled the air and decided it was safe to walk over to the riverside and have a drink. She walked quietly to the water's edge and bent down to drink when suddenly she jumped.

'Oh my goodness,' said Dainty as Freddy the frog leaped into the air.
'Hello,' he said, 'good to see you.'
'Oh you really frightened me,' said Dainty.
'Sorry,' said Freddy. 'It's such a beautiful morning I just thought I'd take some exercise to keep me fit. If you follow me I'll show you where there is some lovely fresh green grass just waiting to be eaten.'
'Thank you,' said Dainty and proceeded to follow Freddy.

As Dainty stood eating she saw Ollie Otter. Dainty asked Ollie if he had seen the people lately.
'Well, no I haven't,' said Ollie, 'but they were chasing Billy and Bella until two smaller people – a boy and a girl – came up to them and made them go away.'
'Who were they?' asked Dainty.
'Well,' said Ollie, 'at our meeting we decided to call them King Terry and Queen Kim, because they helped Billy and Bella. You'll have to talk to the meadow animals. They will tell you all about them.'

'I'll do that, said Dainty, stepping aside from Freddy who was still leaping about like a mad flea.

As Dainty continued to eat the fresh, green grass her thoughts continued to dwell on what Ollie had told her. A king and queen, how nice to have someone to help us when we have problems. I'm glad I live here in Cowslip Corner.

Dainty was also thinking about Freddy leaping about in the morning sun. It's a good job that Kenny Kingfisher isn't here yet or he'd snap Freddy up in a minute. He's only a very small frog.

'Hello Dainty.'
Dainty looked up to see where the voice had come from. It was Red, high up in the treetops, still eating.
'Hello again,' said Dainty. 'It's good to see you. Are you well?'
'I'm very well,' said Red. 'You look a bit thin Dainty, I suppose the winter months were hard on you.'
'Yes they were,' said Dainty. 'I travelled quite a way from here through the woodlands searching for food. It really is hard for us in the wintertime. Some of my friends went to a cottage in the village and they said that a boy and a girl came out to feed them. I would be frightened to do that.'
'You wouldn't be if you were very, very hungry,' said Red. 'Maybe the boy and girl were Terry and Kim. They're our king and queen you know.'
'So I've been told,' said Dainty. 'I must say they sound like very kind people. I think I would still be a little frightened if I met them. Ollie was telling me how good they were to Bella and Billy.'
'That's true,' said Red. 'They really got rid of those awful men

and their dogs. Bella and Billy were so frightened. We felt very sorry for them but what could we do? King Terry and Queen Kim were wonderful. No one is going to bother us while they are our friends are they?'
'No, I shouldn't think so,' said Dainty.

'Quack-quack, quack-quack, quack!'

Dainty looked over towards the river where Davy Duck was swimming. It had been a long time since she had seen him. Davy and Dainty had been born at the same time, exactly two years ago, so they had always been friends. Davy was learning to swim when Dainty's mother had first taken her to the river to drink. Davy had been with his brothers and sisters in the water. His mother had been quacking and telling her brood to swim and search for food just like she did. Davy was the last one to leave the side of the river and go into the deep water. Dainty remembered how small and fluffy he looked and she had felt sorry for him. But everything had been all right and Davy had managed to paddle out to the middle of the river all by himself.

Then, one day, Davy's mother had said 'Bye-bye' and flown away and left all her children but it didn't seem to bother him. They were confident that their mummy had taught them well.

Davy was saying how nice and clean the river was this morning, none of those awful see-through bags in it. Everything was so clear. He could see all the pebbles at the bottom of the river. He hoped it would stay as clean as this in the summertime when the people came.

'Well let's hope so,' said Dainty. 'I really must be going now. I've been standing here talking for ages and ages. It's been so nice to talk to the meadow animals again. I'm looking forward to talking to all the others during the summer too. It's been a long time since I've seen Harry Hedgehog. Is he well?'
'I'm sure he is,' said Davy. 'I know all the meadow animals met the other day. Ollie told me she'd seen him and she would have told me if anything had been wrong. You're bound to see Harry later on in the week. I must go now though.' And off he swam up the river and round the corner until he was completely out of sight.

Dainty sighed and thought that the springtime sun was getting just a little too warm. She decided to go back into the cool woodland and browse amongst the bushes there and with a little skip and a jump she was off into the woods. The only animal who would be able to see her now was Red but he was busy. You know exactly what he was doing. He was eating again!

Well children, you've met most of the animals from Cowslip Corner and I hope you are going to remember their names and follow them in all their adventures with King Terry and Queen Kim.

Late Spring

Chapter One

It was nearing the middle of May. The meadow was a mass of yellow. The cowslips, (or Marsh marigolds), as some people called them, were in full bloom. Marsh means 'wet ground' and patches of the meadow were very wet underneath. This is why there was such green grass mixed with the clover and the buttercups and the cowslips. The meadow looked beautiful. The butterflies loved it and flew around the flowers all day gathering nectar. The meadow animals loved it because there was lots of food for them there. The children loved it too. They would come to the meadow to pick bunches of cowslips and buttercups to take home to their mothers and to watch the butterflies and to try and catch them. The butterflies were always too quick for them. Often Freddy Frog and his brothers and sisters would come out into the meadow in the evening and play underneath the cowslips. Freda liked the cowslips too because, being such tall flowers, she could feel safe hiding behind them where the bigger animals couldn't see her.

Bobby Beaver had finished building his dam. He had a little room under the water with mud and stick walls that kept out the cold. Mrs Beaver was going to have her babies soon so Bobby wanted everything to be ready. Ollie and Olive Otter had a nice nest in the side of the riverbank. They already had three babies. Ollie was so very proud. Poor Davy Duck. Every time they met, all Ollie could talk about was his babies. Davy listened, in order to be polite, and then made some excuse to swim away and rejoin his own family.

The big black crows high up in the treetops had finished building their nests and what a noise they had made! They had been cawing from morning to evening nearly bumping into each other as they flew across the meadow carrying twigs hanging from their beaks. Now the nest building was over it was quieter and soon there would be lots of young crows learning to fly.

Harry hedgehog had been sleeping but was now wide awake sitting in the long grass amongst the flowers washing his face and thinking hedgehog thoughts. The sun was slowly moving over to the west but the butterflies were still in the meadow enjoying feasting on the cowslips. What a beautiful day it had been! Lovely and warm and so peaceful. There had been no people in the meadow today. Not even King Terry or Queen Kim had been to the meadow. Harry started his continual hunt for food meeting many of his friends along the way. They really didn't have much to say to each other. They were all so busy eating and playing in the fading sunlight – just a friendly nod or a smiling 'Hello'. Harry had just stopped to have a little rest and a look around him when Roger Rabbit came hopping by. Roger was smiling.

'Hello,' said Harry. 'What are you looking so pleased about?'
Roger couldn't wait to tell him and the smile on his face was getting bigger and bigger. 'I've met a lovely lady rabbit. Her name is Rosie. Oh Harry, I'm so happy!'
Harry said he was pleased for Roger and said he looked forward to meeting Rosie.
'Oh you will. Quite soon,' said Roger and hopped away with bigger and bigger leaps as he went faster and faster till at last he disappeared through one of the doorways to his burrow.

Harry smiled. He liked to see his friends happy. Sometimes they had a lot of worries especially when the men with the dogs came.

Harry was very thirsty and warm. He decided to go down to the river and have a little drink. He trundled off towards the riverside and began drinking up the cool water from a small, sandy 'beach' nearby. As the water lapped up over his feet he was nearly knocked over by Ollie Otter who was swimming very quickly.

Ollie blew some bubbles and wagged his paw at Harry who knew that Ollie was saying sorry for nearly knocking him over. Ollie carried on swimming weaving here and there in the water and heading out to the middle of the river. Harry also knew though that he probably wouldn't catch the fish who could swim even faster than Ollie but he was having a good game. Even though Ollie was quite fat he was still quick in the water.

Suddenly Ollie turned. It must be his bedtime, thought Harry, and he was right. Ollie swam towards the riverbank, gave a little wave and climbed into a hole. 'That's him gone for the night,' said Harry to himself as he turned and started to walk back across the meadow. Night was coming so quickly. He noticed that most of the birds were quiet now except for a lone blackbird giving out a warning cry. There must be a cat or a dog or people about, he thought as he trundled across the meadow.

Phew! Harry was warm. Everything was so quiet. In the distance he caught a glimpse of Ferdy Fox going into the woods. I wonder if he's had a good day, he thought.

Harry stopped suddenly. He had spotted an absolutely huge slug sliding across the grass in front of him. One jump and Harry had caught it. After washing his face he continued to trundle through the grass. There was so much food around he really didn't have to work hard for his dinner at all. By ten o'clock his tummy was so full that he begun to feel that all he wanted now was his nice comfy bed by the blackberry hedge. He was even beginning to yawn. Harry walked as quickly as he could to his home. When he arrived he saw that on a large clump of cowslips growing near the entrance to his home was a pretty moth curled up fast asleep on the leaves. Harry carefully walked around the cowslips so that he wouldn't wake the moth.

He was having such a job to keep his eyes open. Suddenly something bumped into him. It gave him such a fright that he opened his eyes wide and saw Billy Badger standing in front of him.

'Oh it's you Billy. You did give me a fright.'
'Sorry,' said Billy. 'I'm just heading home. I've been so long talking to Willy weasel that I quite forgot the time and it's got so dark now that I just didn't see you. Sorry for frightening you.'
'It's all right,' said Harry. 'I'm so tired I just didn't see you either. I must learn to be more careful. It is silly of me starting to fall asleep before I got into my bed.'
'Yes,' said Billy. 'You never know if the men and their dogs are about.'
'You're absolutely right. It's very dangerous.' Harry yawned again. 'I must go to bed now. Goodnight.'
'Goodnight,' replied Billy and off he went.

Harry curled himself up into a little ball and in no time at all he was fast asleep dreaming hedgehog dreams.

'Goodnight' said the wind in the trees. 'Goodnight' said the stars. 'Goodnight' said Freddy Frog who was wide awake and having great fun catching tiny night flies that flew around the water. But Harry heard none of this. He was fast asleep. Harry was just a young hedgehog. His older relatives stayed up much later and hunted for food through most of the night. Harry, being a young lad, still had his times a little mixed up, like some young children. Like them he would learn as he got older and by the end of autumn he would probably be getting out of his bed much later in the evening and then returning just before dawn which is the very, very early morning. Right now he was just a bit muddled.

Chapter Two

Dainty woke from a small sleep in the woods to find that a fly had landed on her nose. There was a strange smell in the woodland. Dainty scrambled to her feet and sniffed the air more deeply. The smell was quite strong and she didn't like it at all. It had been a lovely morning too. The sun had shone and Dainty had walked through the woodland stopping every now and then to munch at some of the young leaves that grew on the bushes. She had met Freda Field Mouse when she walked to the edge of the trees. Freda was busy collecting some dried grass to line her nest so her babies would have a cosy bed to sleep in away from the cold of the night air. They had a little chat and while they were talking they looked up and saw Red the squirrel leaping about in the treetops.

'Hello there!' he shouted to them.

'Hello!' they shouted back.

Freda said she must get on and finish her job to be all ready for her babies. Dainty said goodbye and walked back into the middle of the wood keeping a look out all the time for Ferdy Fox. She had always been a little nervous of Ferdy. Although he always appeared very nice and quiet when they met and wasn't rude it was just the way that he looked at her sometimes. She knew she was just being silly. She was bigger than Ferdy and could run faster than him but he didn't talk to her like the other animals did. He really didn't talk to anyone very much. He just prowled about and sniffed around like the big dogs she sometimes saw when they came with the men through the woods. She didn't like them either and she certainly didn't like the men who were very loud and rough looking, not at all like King Terry and Queen Kim.

Sometimes when Dainty was hiding behind a large bush she could see their king and queen walking through the woodland path to Cowslip Corner. She never let them see her though since she was frightened of all the people. Still, they did look nice and happy and they were always careful not to tread on the flowers or break any of the branches on the trees, unlike the men with dogs. The men with the dogs didn't care about the flowers or the trees. They were always hurrying through the woods shouting at the dogs, always looking this way and that as they travelled through. Occasionally they stopped to pick up things from the woodland floor that shone in the sunlight. They would huddle together and talk about what they had gathered. Dainty didn't know what it was that they got since she always kept as far away from them and the dogs as possible.

Again Dainty smelt the air. The smell was different now – it smelt of danger! Dainty started to run but she couldn't escape the smell whichever way she went. Dainty was very frightened. What was it? Then she saw small flames coming out of the low dried grass around the bushes. The woods were on fire. Dainty was terrified. She ran and ran until she was out of breath and then had to stop, panting, her big dark eyes rolling with fear. How could she get away from this awful fire?

Then she heard someone call to her. 'Dainty, Dainty, come this way.'
She looked around but saw no-one.
The voice called again, 'Dainty I'm here.' Dainty looked up and saw Red. 'I'll lead you to safety,' he said. 'Just follow the way I'm going.'
'Alright,' said Dainty and she walked looking up all the time at Red who was leaping from branch to branch showing her a safe route.

Before long Dainty had crossed the stream and the awful smell had faded into the distance. She was safe.

'The fire won't come any further now we've crossed the stream,' said Red. 'I saw what happened from the start. One of the men with dogs threw a match down on the ground on his way through the woods. It's not a bad fire fortunately and it's only the old dried grass that's burning. It should rain tonight, that will put the fire out for good. If it was midsummer it could have been very bad. You must remember the smell though so you'll know to keep well away next time.'
'Yes,' said Dainty, 'I won't forget. Thank you so much for helping me.'

'That's alright. I always try and help my friends, particularly in an emergency. I'm sure you'd do the same. Take care now and have a nice sleep this evening. If you see any of the others tell them about the fire.'

Chapter Three

It had been a warm day again and nothing could be heard in the meadow but the chirping of crickets and the buzzing of bees when, suddenly, there was such a commotion in the hedgerow that it even woke Harry up. He had been fast asleep after a very busy afternoon and evening.

What could it be, thought Harry, and he poked his head out of his nest to have a quick look. Then he saw them. There were two small, scruffy people thrashing the hedgerow with sticks. Harry popped back into his nest again. There was no way he could sleep through with all that noise but he felt safer in his bed. Then he heard the cries of the blackbirds. They had been disturbed.

Oh my goodness, thought Harry, this is horrible. Will they ever go away? Then he heard one of the scruffy people talking.

'Look! There's one. It's got some eggs in it.'
'Cor!' said the other boy. 'I'm gonna get that.'
'Oh no you're not!' said an older, sterner voice. 'Come away from there and leave the birds' nests alone or I'll tell your teacher exactly what you're up to when you should be at school. Drop those sticks and come with me.'

Harry listened, hearing the footsteps of the boys getting quieter and quieter as they moved away from the hedge and out of the meadow. Thank goodness, he thought as he climbed out of his hole again to have a quick look. I wonder who that tall person walking away with those troublesome boys is.

Harry climbed back into his hole, yawned and decided to go back to sleep. It was still so hot outside.

Very soon though, the sun began to dip and the day became cooler. Harry woke again. After stretching and shaking himself he remembered what had happened a short time ago. I wonder if I'll find out what that's all about, he thought to himself as he trundled off again in search of food.

He hadn't been walking very long when he was met by Willy Weasel. Willy was not one of Harry's closest friends. He has such sharp, pointed teeth which scared Harry a little although Willy had always been very nice to Harry.

'Did you see what happened this afternoon?' said Willy.
'I think so. There was that awful noise and what were those two small people trying to do?'

'They were trying to steal the blackbird's eggs,' said Willy. 'Luckily the person who is the father of our king and queen was walking in Cowslip Corner and heard them when they started beating the hedge. The boys were frightened of him because he is a great friend of the school teacher and they should have been at school learning all the things that people do, like reading and writing.'
'Well I'm glad he came,' said Harry, 'because I was scared. Fancy wanting to steal the blackbird's babies. No one would steal other people's babies. We wouldn't would we Willy?'
Willy said nothing to this but shook his tail and said, 'I must be going now, I've got some hunting to do.'
'Well, goodbye then Willy, but I'm going to tell the others about all of this.'

Harry shuffled off again wondering who he would meet next in the meadow. The answer to this came very quickly because Harry was suddenly struck on the head by a flying acorn. Harry looked up. We can all guess who he saw up there can't we? There was Red the squirrel running about in the treetops and chattering like a monkey.

'Hello!' shouted Red. 'I saw everything that happened you know. I don't miss much. They were the boys from the orphanage. They came to take the bird's eggs. They don't have a mother and a father and sometimes they are very naughty because they are unhappy and want attention.'
'How do you know that?' asked Harry. 'You're just a squirrel.'
'I know I'm just a squirrel but I do lots of looking and lots of thinking so I get to know all about these things. I don't spend most of the day sleeping like you do.'
'I have to sleep in the daytime so I can spend the late afternoon

and evening looking for my food. It's really the best time for me.'

'Well I get to see lots of things,' said Red. 'I must see nearly all of the things that happen in Cowslip Corner. I see all the people, the dogs, the cats, the birds and the munchies. I suppose I'm lucky because it's safer for me to stay out and look high up here in the trees where no-one can find me.'

'You're right,' said Harry. 'I suppose you do feel really safe up in the treetops.'

'Certainly,' said Red. 'It's a pity you can't climb up here and come and live with me, but then again, you'd probably fall out of your bed.'

Harry laughed. 'You're right again,' he said. 'I think I'd better stay in my home beneath the blackberry hedge.'

Chapter Four

The black and white pony came galloping down the road at such a fast pace and jumped over the hedge where the stile was. She was panting heavily and sweat covered her coat and dripped down from around her mouth. She landed knee-deep in the long grass of Cowslip Corner. Red of course saw her arrive and so did Billy Badger, Kenny Kingfisher and Roger Rabbit. The pony stood still after her jump, shook herself and looked around. After a while she bent her head down and started to eat some of the lovely green grass that grew in the meadow. A few minutes passed and then the watching animals saw King Terry and Queen Kim climbing over the stile. They carried on watching. This was unusual. They had never had a pony in the meadow before. What was she doing in their home? They all sat very still and watched and listened. King Terry was talking to Queen Kim as they walked slowly over to where the pony was grazing.

'You shouldn't have let go of her until you had put the halter around her neck,' said King Terry.
'Oh Terry, I was just hugging her. She seemed so frightened. All those cuts all over her back and being so thin, I just wanted to give her a little love.'
'That's nice,' said Terry, 'but you know she's very frightened after the way she's been treated. We have to be very careful with her because she doesn't know us yet. She probably thinks we'll hurt her like the people who used to own her.'
'She should know we won't.'
'How should she know?' said King Terry as he began to walk towards the pony slowly and carefully.

The pony stood looking at king Terry and Queen Kim. The animals thought she looked as though she was going to run away again but King Terry gently put the halter around her neck quietly talking to her all the time.

'Come on my beauty,' he said. 'We won't hurt you. Daddy is going to make you better and Kim and I are going to take care of you. You'll never have to go back to those awful people again. You're going to live with us. There's a good girl. Come on, let's take you home and put you in the barn for the night. You'll soon get used to us.
The pony lifted her head and neighed.
'I think she understands,' said Kim.
'Yes, I do too,' answered Terry.

King Terry and Queen Kim walked slowly away with the pony. They had to go through the woods and then along a small track that went out on to the road. The animals of Cowslip Corner watched hoping that now they had a pony to look after, King Terry and Queen Kim wouldn't forget all of them.

Terry and Kim walked up the woodland path holding the pony close to them.

'I think she knows we're her friends now,' said Terry.
'What shall we call her?' asked Kim.
'I think we should name her Beauty,' said Terry.
'Oh that's a lovely name,' said Kim. 'Come on Beauty, we're going home now. When you've got used to living with us a little more we'll ask Daddy if you can go into the meadow again and eat all that lovely fresh grass and you can get to know all our friends in Cowslip Corner.'
Beauty neighed again. She seemed happy now she was beginning to trust Terry and Kim.

After a while they arrived at the barn and Terry gave Beauty a large bucket of cool water and a bale of hay to eat. The barn was warm and cosy.

'She'll be fine tonight,' said Terry.
'Yes,' said Kim. 'I'll just give her a kiss goodnight like Mummy and Daddy give us when we go to bed. She'll feel like one of the family then.'
'I think that would be nice,' said Terry.

The children both kissed Beauty goodnight, locked the barn door and strode up the path to their house.

Their mother and father knew they were excited and that it

had been a busy day for them getting to know Beauty, brushing her down and taking her out for some exercise. When the children came in Mummy had their tea ready for them and the bath was filled ready for them to go to bed and dream about the day they had just had. The children barely managed to eat their tea and walk up the stairs to bed.

'Goodnight Terry.'
'Goodnight Kim. Isn't Beauty lovely. I'm glad we found her.'
Kim didn't answer though. She was fast asleep.

They remembered how yesterday Beauty had been brought to see their father at the vets. The correct name for a vet is 'veterinary surgeon' as their father had told them.

He had been a vet for a long time and the children had often been to visit him at his surgery. The lady who had brought Beauty in had been very upset. She had explained that she had found the pony wandering down the road in a terrible state. She had lots of cuts and was so thin and dirty. She had been ill-treated by her owners and she had run away. Terry and Kim's father had phoned the RSPCA, (the Royal Society for the Prevention of Cruelty to Animals), to try and find the people who had been so horrible to Beauty.

The lady who had brought Beauty in nodded in agreement when the children's father said, 'It's absolutely dreadful the way some people treat animals.'

Unfortunately the lady couldn't take Beauty back with her. She didn't have enough room to keep her properly. She said, 'I hope you can find a good home for her.'

'I think we could take her in. I know Terry and Kim would love a pony and I know they would look after her properly.'

The lady thanked him and left. The children's father set about bathing all the cuts on the pony's back and giving her a good meal. 'We'll have you looking good again in no time.'

After he had applied some ointment to the cuts he rang the house and told Terry and Kim's mother all about the pony.

'She'll have to stay in the barn tonight,' he said. 'We won't tell the children about her today. Let's wait until tomorrow and give them a real surprise. They'll be so happy to have their own pony. I know they'll love taking her down to Cowslip Corner to meet all their animal friends.'
'I can't wait to see their faces,' said Mother. 'I bet they spoil the pony!'

The news about the pony was soon all over the meadow. Red and Roger had been telling all the other animals.
'I hope she won't kick me or stand on me,' said Freda Field Mouse.
'Ponies aren't stupid you know. They can see and hear too,' said Red.

Freda Field Mouse rushed away though, still worried but she had lots of work to do so soon her mind was far away on other matters.

'She won't bother me,' said Roger.
'Or me,' said Red. 'She can't climb trees. She won't bother Ollie, Olive, Billy or Bella either. We'd better warn Harry

though. He might frighten the pony when he's shuffling around at night.'

'I'll tell him,' said Roger. 'I'm always meeting him.'

'OK,' said the others. 'Make sure that you do.'

Roger hopped away, eager to get back to his family again. Willie Weasel had been listening too. The pony won't bother me either, he thought and ran quickly into the hedgerow.

Harry had missed all this conversation and all the excitement. He had been sleeping the whole time but no doubt Harry would meet Beauty. Who knows? They might even become very good friends.

Back in the barn Beauty yawned. She was very sleepy and for the first time in her life she felt safe and happy. She had begun to trust the two young children who had been with her and hoped that she would be able to stay with them for ever and ever. They were so kind to her, not at all like the horrible people she was kept by before. They had been cruel to her and sometimes they didn't feed her at all. If she couldn't pull the cart they tied her to they would whip her. She had been so unhappy that she had decided to run away. One night when they had left her tied to a tree by a rope she pulled so hard that the rope broke and she ran off. She had been found by the kind lady the next morning.

After a long and restful sleep, Beauty stood in the barn thinking about all the things that had happened to her. I really do feel happy now, she thought. I wonder if I will be able to stay with these kind people?

'Too-whit-a-woo, too-whit-a-woo.'

Beauty turned around. What a strange noise, she thought. Where did it come from? She stood looking at the floor of the barn. There was nothing there that could have made the noise, only clean straw and a bucket of water.

Then she looked at the walls of the barn all painted nice and white with just a saddle and a harness hanging from an iron hook by the door. That wasn't making the noise either.

Next Beauty looked up at the roof of the barn. Big wooden beams of oak stretched from wall to wall under the roof. Beauty could see some spiders' webs but spiders didn't make that kind of a noise.

Suddenly Beauty spotted a small bird, an owl. Owls are birds that come out at night to find their food and Beauty had not seen one before. Beauty stood looking up at the small bird.

'Too-whit-a-woo,' it said again, looking back at Beauty. 'Are you my new friend? It does get so lonely in here sometimes with no-one to talk to.'
'Yes,' said Beauty. 'I'll be your friend. I've never had any friends before though.'
'Oh that's horrible! I have friends but I only see them when I go out of the barn to hunt. Sometimes we all sit on a tree branch and have a good old chat about everything that has happened to us but here in the barn it's so quiet. Most of the time I'm sleeping but when I'm not I've often thought it would be nice to have someone to talk to.'

'Well I'd love to talk to you,' replied Beauty. 'I was just thinking how much I'd like to stay here. I was so unhappy before when I was kept by some really horrible people but the boy and girl who took me home from the meadow do seem so kind.'
'You must mean King Terry and Queen Kim,' said Barn Owl. 'I'd heard they were in the meadow earlier with a pony. They really are nice people and they are so kind to the animals. We all feel so much safer in Cowslip Corner knowing they are looking out for us.'
'Where's Cowslip Corner?' asked Beauty.
'That's the meadow they brought you home from. I was told that you'd jumped over the stile like a champion racehorse!'

Beauty put her head down and looked a little ashamed.

'Well, yes I did.' She said. 'I was still frightened and I didn't know where I was or what was going to happen to me. I was worried that the people I used to belong to were going to come and fetch me and I didn't want that. I'd really like to live in Cowslip Corner though. Everyone seems so friendly.'
'Yes. We like to help each other out when we can. My name's Barney by the way. There are lots of friendly animals in Cowslip Corner like Harry, Roger, Billy, Kenny and Freddy and lots more besides. You will have to be careful though. Some of the people aren't so friendly when they come around with the big dogs. King Terry got rid of them for us last time but I'm sure they'll be back.'
'I'll kick them if they come near me.'
'That's the spirit,' said Barney. 'I'm sure you'll be fine. You're bigger than all the other animals and everyone will be pleased to know that you're going to be our friend. King Terry and Queen Kim call you Beauty don't they?'

'Do they? I like that name.'
'Goodnight then Beauty.'
'Goodnight Barney.'

Beauty soon fell asleep after such a busy and exciting day and dreamt beautiful dreams just like Harry always did.

Summer

Chapter One

What a hot day it had been! The sun had shone continuously and not a cloud in the sky. Harry snoozed in the cool shade of the hedgerow. Kenny snoozed in the tree by the river. Freda stayed down in her little nest and Red was napping in the shade of a dense patch of leaves in the top of a large oak tree. But Ollie, Olive and Freddy Frog were in the best place for keeping cool. They were all swimming or jumping about in the beautiful clear water. Beauty stood at the side of the meadow under the shade of the woodland trees, just flicking her tail now and again to keep the flies away. Even the small birds sat in the trees and the big crows were very quiet for a change – they were probably snoozing too!

The meadow had not been so peaceful earlier though! Mothers had been taking advantage of the lovely weather and had brought their children out for picnics. They had been splashing about in the shallow water of the river enjoying themselves tremendously. It was the summer holidays when the children didn't have to go to school and they were all so excited to have a day in the meadow, and a picnic too!

Most of the children had been very well behaved and had listened to what their mothers had told them about respecting animals' homes. But there were some who were not. Their mothers didn't seem to bother about what they were doing. They gave the children food wrapped in see-through bags which the children then left scattered around the meadow. Some of them left empty lemonade cans too.

Sometimes their mothers would go to sleep in the warm sunshine and then there would be no one to make sure that the children behaved. Then the children, being children, did exactly what they wanted to do and they ran around the meadow shouting and yelling, pulling the grass up and throwing it at each other. They even started trying to catch the frogs by the side of the river and they frightened Beauty by dancing around her. Suddenly Beauty neighed very loudly and galloped away which scared the children so they didn't go near her again.

Eventually they all went home and the meadow became quiet

again. But what a mess they had left behind. It was only four young children who had been irresponsible and made a mess of the meadow but they had left it in such a state! There were patches where the grass had been worn or pulled away, empty cans and those awful see-through bags over the place. Beauty was all anxious and trying to keep herself cool and the frogs still didn't dare come out of the shallow water. It was peaceful now though. Evening was coming and it brought a cool breeze blowing through the woodland trees.

It was the chill of the breeze that woke Harry up. When he woke he trundled out to the meadow but he couldn't believe his little eyes. When he had gone to bed he had left a lovely clean, green meadow but now it was such a mess! There were tin cans and tufts of grass and those dreadful see-through bags blowing about all over the place. Well, thought Harry, at least the wind will soon blow those away. Harry was right because the wind did blow the bags away but it blew some of the bags into the field where the munchies were grazing and some blew into the river too.

The sky became darker and Harry started out on his constant search for food. He didn't see any of his friends except Beauty and some tiny bats flying overhead. But he did hear one of the munchies mooing very loudly although he thought nothing of it and just trundled along enjoying himself. The moon soon came out and it cast a pale, cool light over the woodland trees and the meadow. How pretty my home is, thought Harry, we're all so lucky to be living in Cowslip Corner. I wonder where King Terry and Queen Kim are. We haven't seen them for such a long time.

Well, it so happened that Terry and Kim were on holiday at the seaside with their mummy and daddy. They had been there for two whole weeks and although they had enjoyed themselves they were anxious to get back to Cowslip Corner and be with Beauty and all the other animals. Tomorrow they would be home and the very first thing they would do, when they had finished all their jobs for Mummy and Daddy, would be to walk along the woodland path to Cowslip Corner. Right at the moment when Harry was thinking about them, they were tucked up in bed in their hotel whispering to each other about coming home.

'Just think,' said Terry, 'we'll be back in the meadow tomorrow. I bet Beauty will be pleased to see us.'
'Yes,' said Kim. 'Just like we'll be pleased to see her and the meadow and the river and all the other animals.'

The munchies were really fed-up with the hot weather. The grass was getting dry and the water in the river was very low. But most of all they were sad because one of their dear friends, Blossom, had been taken away by the farmer. Blossom had been quite all right the day before when all those people had come to the meadow. She had swished her tail watching the people in the meadow running, eating and listening to the music. It had been very noisy and busy but Blossom had enjoyed looking at new things for a change and she was constantly flicking her long eyelashes over her big brown eyes. Blossom was a very friendly Munchie. She had had two babies but they had been taken away to other farms a long time ago. The farmer was always praising her for the milk she gave him.

When the farmer came to take her away the other munchies

just couldn't understand it. They had been talking about it amongst themselves ever since.

One munchie said, 'I heard Blossom making a terrible noise during the night. She was mooing and mooing. She sounded terribly distressed as though she had something caught in her throat. I asked her if she was alright and she said she had swallowed something that caught in her throat but that it was alright now. Whatever it was must have made her ill this morning.'
The other munchies nodded and returned to looking for the small patches of green grass.

Roger had seen what had happened. He had been sitting outside one of the many entrances to his home chewing a dried up piece of carrot that he'd found in the farmer's field. He'd seen Blossom move over to a tall clump of grass. Roger also saw a shiny see-through bag crumpled in the grass. He saw her munch for a bit before coughing and moving away making a horrendous sound with her coughing. Roger wasn't sure what had happened but couldn't check because just then there was a large 'Bang, bang' in the sky. Roger ran but not before he saw two birds fall from the sky. Roger was terrified. He scuttled down his tunnel and kept running till he was back in Cowslip Corner. Things like that don't happen in Cowslip Corner.

'Phew', he said when he was safe. 'That was a close one. I think I had better stay in the woods and the meadow now, it's much safer. I wonder if those two birds bumped into something in the sky? They made such a noise as if they did. I'm glad I can't fly!'

So passed another hot summer day. Luckily Harry had been sleeping through all this bother in his cool, quiet home by the blackberry hedge. At about five o'clock that evening King Terry and Queen Kim arrived to sit by the side of the very shallow river.

They looked out for a while and then Terry said, 'Daddy told me that another munchie had swallowed a plastic bag.'
'Oh that's terrible,' said Kim. 'Can't something be done about people leaving them all over the meadow?'
'It's very difficult,' said Terry. 'As long as no-one owns this piece of land anyone is free to do exactly what they want to do. In fact, in the woods next to the munchies' field a man was shooting birds the other day.'
Kim started to cry. 'I wish you wouldn't tell me things like that.'
'But, it's true,' said Terry.
'People are coming here from the town and some of them just don't care what kind of damage they do. If Cowslip Corner belonged to me I'd only let my friends in and people that were kind to the animals and the birds,' said Kim.
'It doesn't though,' said Terry, 'and we'll never own it. There's nothing we could do about it. We don't have enough money to buy a meadow and a woodland. Land is very expensive.'
'I know,' said Kim, 'but wouldn't it be lovely if it was really ours?'
'Yes it is a nice dream,' said Terry. 'Come on. We'd better be getting home now. Mummy and Daddy will be worrying.'

Chapter Two

A stillness had come over the meadow, the woods and the river. The sky was a dark blue with small clouds dotted here and there and just the occasional burst of music of a thrush singing and crickets chirping in the background. The water in the river was still. Occasionally a small fish bobbed to the surface making a tiny ripple. Apart from these things all was quiet. Was everyone home and sleeping? The animals of Cowslip Corner were doing the things they always did, looking for food and playing. A quiet had fallen over the meadow though as the skies became darker and all the animals knew that there was going to be a rainstorm. There had been a strong breeze earlier but now it was still – so still. Not a single blade of grass was moving.

The frog family knew exactly what was going to happen. The

sky would become darker still and the rain would absolutely pour down. They were getting excited – especially the young frogs waiting for it to start raining.

The rain started slowly. Spit, spat, spot. Large drops of water fell from the sky. The grass in the munchies' field looked up towards the sky, just waiting for a drink and the munchies gathered at the edge of the field under the branches of the woodland trees. The thrushes stopped singing and there was nothing to be heard from the crickets.

Rain, beautiful rain making everything green again. Green and clean. The young frogs were jumping and jumping. They croaked out to each other. What a super game they were having jumping onto the sticks that were floating in the water or onto some of the larger stones that were submerged in the shallow water at the river's edge.

One little frog was standing on a piece of a tree branch (he thought) and floating down the river so fast that he cried 'Help, help' to his brothers and sisters. They all looked round and begun to laugh.

'Look at our little brother!' they all shouted. 'He's jumped onto Betty beaver's back by mistake. He thinks he's on a piece of wood. Betty will be going under the water soon to get to her dam. Come on silly brother. Hop off now or you'll be stuck in the middle of the river.'

They all turned round and looked at their little brother croaking for him to jump. Poor little frog! He was so frightened he couldn't jump.

Luckily Betty had noticed that something wasn't quite right. There was something heavy on her back. She looked round just as she was about to dive under the water.

Oh my goodness, she thought, I can't take this little frog with me. He'll get lost and then he'll never find his own family again. She turned around and headed back off to the riverbank. She really was a kind beaver.

All the other frogs were watching and becoming more and more worried about their little brother.

'Oh look!' cried one of them. Betty Beaver is coming over here.'

Betty was swimming so fast that all the other frogs had to jump out of the way but she slowed down as she approached the riverbank and gently swam to the shallow water at the edge. She turned and looked at the little frog.

'Come on now. Get off my back and go and find your brothers and sisters,' she said.

The little frog thanked her. He was so glad that Betty had been so kind to him that he leapt into the air as high as he could and landed on the riverbank with a thud! All his family jumped over to him.

'You've learned a lesson today,' said his mother. 'The people have a saying for it – look before you leap, they say.'
'Oh I certainly will from now on,' said the little frog and he

jumped off once more to rejoin his brothers and sisters in the reeds that grew by the riverbank. He was so tired from all his adventures that he fell asleep.

Just as the little frog fell asleep, Harry was waking up. It was evening now and Harry's thoughts immediately turned to finding more food in the tall, wet, juicy grass of the meadow.

Chapter Three

When Harry woke up his eyes did a funny thing. They crossed! Something was on the end of his nose. He sneezed and it flew away. It was a butterfly.

Fancy having a butterfly on the end of my nose, thought Harry, it must have been there for a long time. Anyway, I must go off and look for my dinner.

Ferdy Fox smelled the air and turned to his wife, 'You can bring the cubs out now,' he said.

Ferdy, his wife and five cubs slowly and carefully came out of the woods but the cubs wouldn't be careful for very long. They had to play, jumping and running, catching each other's tails and yapping. Their mother was beginning to get worried.

'Be quiet you silly little things. Don't you know you have to be quiet and learn to hunt and keep out of the way of people. The people are always looking for us and hunting us. If you make all that noise and stop being careful and off your guard all the time the people will find you very quickly and take you away. You must always listen to me and keep close by me.'

The little cubs stopped their playing and gathered by their mother's side, all except one. He was busy chasing a moth that was flying amongst the tall grass.

'Do come here,' said his mother. 'Will you not learn to listen to me and come here when I call you.'
The little cub tucked his tail under his legs and rejoined the others. Then they all walked slowly and silently across the meadow.

Harry watched them till they disappeared from view. I hope they always listen to their mother, he thought, else they'll be in trouble.

The fox family continued through the woods with Fenella (that was the mother fox's name) checking constantly and calling the cubs to her side. But number five cub was such a naughty little cub that he was always the last to come when his mother called and was always the furthest away from the rest of the family. He didn't mean to be naughty, he just liked to explore and look at everything in the forest – the large trees, the big green ferns that grew underneath them, the pretty flowers and anything else that was unusual to him – number five just had to have a look at it.

Just like some children he would have many lessons to learn about growing up and being careful of things he didn't know about, but right now he didn't worry about anything at all. He just ran here and there playfully looking at everything curious just like a puppy dog.

Ferdy and his family walked on and on through the now dark woodland. Mrs Fox stopped to count her cubs.

'Oh dear!' she said. 'Where is number five? He's gone missing again,'
The other four little cubs started to cry.
'Don't cry, said Mrs Fox. 'You make a lot of noise when you cry. Let's be very careful, stay together and we'll look for number five.'
The other four cubs agreed and stopped crying. They followed their mummy and daddy back up the woodland trail very quietly. Suddenly an awful cry sounded through the woods.

'Oh my goodness,' said Mrs Fox. 'That was number five! Something has happened to him.'

They all rushed off in the direction that the cry had come from. They found number five in some bushes with his tail trapped in a man-trap. He was crying and crying.

'What shall we do?' cried the cubs.
'There's nothing we can do,' said their father. Then they heard a dog howling in the distance, coming from the direction of the village. 'Now the men will come.'
'I will have to stay with my baby,' said the mother as they began to hear the sound of footsteps coming along the path.

They all stood still and watched.

Davy Duck was flapping and quacking, swimming round and round in circles. He was so upset. Where was everyone? Where were his friends? Last night there had been the most awful commotion and noise from the woods. It was a beautiful moonlit night earlier on and Davy had been awake. He shouldn't have been awake but his wife Dilly and his children had been fidgeting all night. The children were only three days old and Dilly was worn out taking care of them and teaching them to swim and look for their own food. It was very hard work and she wasn't such a big duck herself but such a good mummy to her ducklings. At night time she had them all tucked under her wing on a dry shelf of earth by the river. But they were so fidgety! They were always trying out their 'Quacks' and flapping their little wings. They were all so excited about all the new things they had seen and done in the daytime that it had taken them such a long time to get to sleep.

And they had woken Davy up! He didn't really mind though because the river looked so pretty and the light from the moon made it look just like daytime. Davy had slipped into the water and sat there looking at the sky, the stars and the meadow when suddenly he had heard such an awful cry. It had come from the woods. The woods looked so dark now even though the moon was shining brightly. Of course Davy couldn't see through the darkness of the trees. But he knew that the cry had come from the woods. Was it Dainty? Had something happened to her? Then he heard the cry again. Davy was worried and very sad. Something awful had happened in the dark woods. Davy swam up the river to the side of the woodland trees. He heard the cry again but this time there were different sounds too. People sounds. He stopped swimming and listened. It was King Terry and Queen Kim. What were they doing in the woods at this time of night he wondered.

Everything suddenly became quiet. There was not a sound. Davy looked around. All he saw was the big, white moon and bats flying low by the trees. I hope nothing has happened to my friends, thought Davy.

Of course now Davy couldn't sleep. He just had to wait until morning to find out what had happened. He sat by the edge of the water hoping and waiting to see someone and talk about the events of the night. As he sat worrying there was a swish in the water beside him and Ollie Otter poked his head up.

'Oh my goodness,' said Davy because Ollie had given him quite a fright. 'Do you know what was going on last night?'
'Not really,' replied Ollie, 'just that there was a terrible commotion in the woods.

Then Roger Rabbit came hopping along. 'You should be glad you weren't in the woods like I was last night,' he said. 'It was horrible. There I was all tucked up in bed with my family around me when there was this terrible cry. I rushed out of my bedroom so I could see into the woods and I saw one of Ferdy Fox's little ones caught in a trap set by some of the people. He was crying and crying but I felt so helpless. I couldn't do anything to help him. Ferdy came up with his wife and they all started howling and the noise was awful! The bats were flying overhead and they all started squeaking. Then a dog began howling in the village and then I heard some people talking. The sound of the people got nearer and nearer and then I saw a light through the trees. Guess who it was. It was King Terry and Queen Kim. They were dressed in funny clothes. King Terry had a light with him which he shone onto the trap which had the little cub in it. Queen Kim started to cry too but King Terry told her not to but to help him free the little cub. They both knelt down on the grass and managed to get that awful trap open. Luckily the cub had only been caught by his tail and although he was hurt and very scared he hadn't broken any bones. I could see Ferdy and the rest of his family hiding in the bushes while all this was going on. Ferdy could see that his little one was in safe hands. King Terry handed the cub to Queen Kim and said that he would take the trap to show the police. They left taking the cub with them. They said they were going to take him to their father to make him better. They wondered if the cub's family would miss him and if they would understand he was now in safe hands.'

When Roger had finished telling his story Davy Duck said, 'Oh my goodness! What a terrible thing to happen! I'm glad it wasn't me or any of my family.'
'So am I,' said Ollie Otter and quickly swam away.

Davy felt that he'd just like a little sleep so he paddled back to where his family were. 'Quack, quack' he said quietly before he closed his eyes. He knew he wouldn't have a very long sleep as the ducklings would be awake very soon flapping about and practising their quacking. Davy fell asleep just as the rest of the meadow animals were waking up. Except Harry of course. He was still in a dreamless sleep.

Chapter Four

Whoosh! Whoosh! Kenny Kingfisher had arrived. He swooped down to a big willow tree and settled himself on a branch overhanging the river. Kenny had been in a hurry to get back to his favourite place in Cowslip Corner and was eager to see his friends again and listen to their chattering. He heard a noise in the grass behind him and turned round to see Freda Field Mouse looking at him.

'Hello Freda,' said Kenny.
'Hello Kenny,' she replied. 'Can't stop. I'm very busy, just like a bee.'

Kenny turned round again and sat looking at the still water. As he sat watching some ripples broke the surface of the water. What's this, he thought. Then Davy Duck and his family came swimming round the bend in the river.

'Hello Kenny,' shouted Davy.
'Hello ducks,' shouted Kenny. He smiled to himself as he noticed how proud Davy was of his family. They were pretty little ducklings too. Kenny preened his feathers and settled down to wait for his breakfast. The sun had come out and the birds had started to sing. I bet I'll see Red soon, he thought.

'Hello,' came a call from the woodland trees. 'how are you Kenny?'
'I'm fine Red,' and Kenny swooped down from his perch to the river where he had seen a fish bobbing about by the surface. Olive Otter had seen the fish too but Kenny had beaten her to it.
'I think I'll go down the river a little way. You're much too quick for me Kenny,' said Olive and swam off to find her own breakfast.

Kenny settled himself again to wait for another fish. He was glad to be back in Cowslip Corner.

As Kenny sat on the tree branch preening himself and feeling very pleased that he was back, he glanced slowly across the meadow. Oh good! It's still the same as I remember – it hasn't changed a bit. But just then he saw a large, dark shape standing by the hedgerow around where the blackberries grew. What's that? he thought. That wasn't here before. I'll have to go and investigate. It's not Harry and it's not Ollie or Freda either. It can't be any of my friends unless one of them has grown extremely tall since I've been away.'

Kenny stretched up and spread his wings and carefully flew over to where the large shape was standing.

Beauty blinked her eyes and swished her tail. Who on earth is that large, blue bird? she thought.

Kenny swooped down until he was just above her head. 'Hello,' he said. 'I've not see you here before. Have you been here very long? Do King Terry and Queen Kim know you are here?'
Beauty looked up at Kenny. 'Of course they do,' she neighed. 'They brought me here. I've met all the animals in Cowslip Corner but I've never seen you before.'
'No, you wouldn't have,' replied Kenny. 'I must have left before you arrived. I'm sorry if I frightened you. My name is Kenny Kingfisher. I spend most of my time in one of the trees by the river looking for fish.'
'I'm pleased to meet you Kenny. My name is Beauty. King Terry and Queen Kim brought me here earlier in the summer.'
'I'm not usually this late back. I got held up by a terrible storm on my way here and thought it best to stop and wait until the storm had passed and it was safe for me to fly high up in the sky again.'
'That sounds sensible,' said Beauty. 'You might have been driven down out of the sky and hurt yourself and some bad people might have found you and tried to put you in a cage.'

Kenny thought Beauty was very wise and that she would be a good friend to him and all the others in Cowslip Corner.

'I'm glad to have met you, Beauty,' he said. 'I must go now though and find some more breakfast and I feel tired after all that flying so I think I'll have a little sleep.'

'I'm pleased to have met you too. Have a nice day and we'll meet again some time and chat. Goodbye for now,' said Beauty.

Kenny flew back to his favourite branch by the river. How nice, he thought. Fancy having a pony as a friend. She'll be such a help to all the animals in Cowslip Corner. With that Kenny fell asleep. Don't worry though children. Birds don't fall off branches when they go to sleep.

The sky was blue and the birds were all singing. All the animals were up and about except Harry and Kenny who were both fast asleep. Red had seen Kenny arrive and was just itching to talk to him but realised that he'd still be tired after his long journey.

All the frogs were settled under the tall rushes by the riverside. Their mummies and daddies had warned them about Kenny: 'He might think you're a fish by mistake if you go hopping about in the water,' they said. 'You'll be alright at night time because he'll be asleep. You'd better be quiet until this evening.' The little frogs did as they were told because they knew that their parents knew best.

Davy, Dilly and the little ducklings came swimming by again. Davy quacked at Kenny to say hello but it was no use, Kenny was fast asleep. Davy paddled on again having decided to wait until tomorrow.

Dainty was dozing in the cool of the woodland and Ferdy and his family were taking things easy too. Things were very calm in Cowslip Corner but when Harry wakes up some more things are bound to happen.

Late Summer

Chapter One

Roger, Red and Kenny were wide awake. It had barely become light. Roger was the first to hear the noise. He always woke early so he could be out in the fields and hedgerows searching for food. Sometimes he even went quite close to the road in case a person had done something they shouldn't and had thrown something out of their car as they were travelling. Often it was left-over food. Roger had learnt about this and sometimes found quite tasty bits and pieces.
However, today when he awoke he heard a noise and it was

such a noise that it seemed to shake the ground over his tunnel. Whatever was it? Roger was a little frightened so he didn't rush out of his tunnel straight away to have a look but slowly looked around and chose the tunnel passage nearest to where the awful noise was coming from.

When he got to the opening in the meadow he looked around and saw Kenny flapping his wings just like a crazy kingfisher. Then he saw Red in the treetops running from branch to branch chattering away.

'What is it?' shouted Roger. 'This noise is going to wake up all my children and my wife.'
'Look over at the munchies' field,' shouted Red. 'If you look you'll see Blossom. She's back. Isn't that wonderful?'

Roger looked over to the munchies' field and there, surrounded by all the other munchies who had been mooing and mooing, stood Blossom.

'How lovely to see her again,' said Roger. 'Is that what all the noise was about?'
'Yes!' shouted Red. 'The munchies are all so happy to see her again and so am I.'
'Well I am too,' said Roger.

Kenny flew down to where Roger stood. 'I'm so excited to see Blossom again,' he said. 'They told me that the farmer person took her away so I didn't think we'd ever see her again. I can't wait to tell the others in Cowslip Corner.'
'Me too!' shouted Red.
'Me as well!' shouted Roger, who was very, very pleased but

now he was thinking that someone else may have got to the right side of the road and found some tasty meals before he'd had a chance to look for himself. Ferdy might have been there already with his brood. 'I'm off!' he shouted. 'I've got some important things to do.'

Red and Kenny knew exactly where Roger was going. They watched him every morning hopping across the meadow to the side of the road. It worried them a little that one day Roger would go too far along that road and that a fast car would come speeding along and Roger would be so interested in the food that he wouldn't see it coming.'
'I hope he'll be careful,' said Red.
'Me too,' said Kenny. 'He's getting a little too bold. He should keep away from that nasty road. Let the people stay there. He should stay in the meadow and the woods.'
'Well he's still young,' said Red. 'Maybe he'll learn a lesson and be more careful.'
'I hope so,' said Kenny. 'Well I'm off now to look for my breakfast.'
'Cheerio,' said Red and ran to the very top of the tree to find some of his acorns which he'd hidden in a hole so high up that he just knew no one else would find them.

Well that was exciting, thought Red. It's so nice that Blossom is back. It's going to be a good day today, I just know it!

Freda had been sitting listening to Roger, Red and Kenny. She too was happy that Blossom was back. Wait till King Terry and Queen Kim see her, she thought, maybe they asked the farmer person to bring her back.
But that wasn't the way things had happened.

Chapter Two

Danielle and Matthew had been very unhappy. They were the farmer person's children but they were grown-up children now. Danielle was married and even had a baby girl. Matthew worked in the big city but they had brought Blossom up since she was a tiny calf and her mother had died. They had known Blossom all of her young life and they loved her very much.

'Why are you taking her away?' asked Danielle. 'She's done nothing wrong. She can't always give a lot of milk, especially as she's getting older now. She's still our baby though and we should be able to say whether she stays here or has to go away.'

Danielle had started crying by now.

'She swallowed one of those plastic bags,' said their father.

'She's no use to me now. It'll cost a lot of money to make her better and she might not even be able to give me any more milk.'

'I don't care about that,' said Matthew. 'We'll pay for anything that has to be done to save Blossom. Can't you understand we love her. Just because those stupid people threw their bags away in Cowslip Corner and Blossom swallowed one, why should she suffer? We're going to take her to the vet. He'll make her better. We don't mind what we have to pay, just as long as Blossom gets better and you'll let her live near Cowslip Corner again.'

The farmer person nodded. 'Alright,' he said. 'We'll take her to the vet tomorrow. I just hope that the vet can get the plastic bag out of her tummy.'

'I'm sure he will,' said Danielle. 'He's a very clever vet.'

The next morning they all set off taking Blossom, who wasn't feeling at all well, to the vet. They drove there in a big truck with Blossom in the back. Danielle stayed with Blossom in the back because she knew she would be afraid of the truck's engine not knowing where she was going or what was going to happen to her. Danielle sat with her arms around Blossom talking quietly to her.

'We're going to take you to a man who will make you better,' she told her. 'Matthew and I will always love you. We know you'll get better and then you can go back to Cowslip Corner and spend all your days there.'

When they arrived at the surgery the vet, who was a friend of the farmer, said 'I'll operate on her straight away. If only those stupid people realised what they were doing when they throw these things away. They are a danger to many animals. Another big problem I have is the birds who are brought in with fishing lines tangled around their beaks and down their throats. I just wish people would be more careful when they go to the countryside.'

The farmer agreed, said goodbye to the vet, and left but Danielle and Matthew stayed behind. They wanted to be with Blossom when the vet operated on her. The vet said that it would be alright.

Blossom was very frightened as the vet came towards her with the large needle in his hand. 'I'm not going to hurt you,' he said. 'There'll just be a small prick and then you'll go to sleep and I'll be able to get that nasty thing out of your tummy.'
No sooner had the vet finished saying that than Blossom began to close her big brown eyes and fall asleep.
'Right then,' said the vet, 'let's start and make Blossom better.'

About an hour afterwards all was finished. Blossom was still sleeping but the vet had done his work well and all the twisted up plastic bag had been removed from her tummy. All Blossom had now was a big scar underneath.

'That won't take long to heal,' said the vet. 'She's a healthy cow, she'll be with you for many more years.'

Matthew and Danielle hugged the vet. They were so happy that there hadn't been any complications and Blossom would get well.

'Come back and collect her in a couple of days,' the vet told them. 'She'll be looking forward to getting back with all the other munchies.'

So you see children. That explains why Blossom is back in the field with all of her friends and why they had made such a noise to greet her. As Red had said, it was a very nice day today!

Chapter Three

The morning passed and by the time the sun was shining brightly in Cowslip Corner all the animals, except Harry of course who was still asleep, knew that Blossom was back. They all nodded to each other and said how very pleased they were when they met. As it was now late summer, all the families of animals had their babies to look after. Olive and Ollie had four little cubs, Betty and Bobby had six young beavers all looking like large kittens and Davy Duck and his wife Dilly had their eight little ducklings flapping around them all day and all night. Even Roger and his pretty wife Rosie had had their babies. Roger was so very proud. His youngsters were so tiny that they hadn't been out into Cowslip Corner yet. They were still only two days old and Rosie had been with them all the time in one of their small rooms under the ground. We know that Ferdy had some cubs too don't we? Number five had that terrible experience with the trap.

It was such a beautiful day and more good things were going to happen. Can you guess? That's right. King Terry and Queen Kim are going to bring number five cub back to Cowslip Corner today. They didn't call him Number Five though. Terry and Kim had renamed him 'Fluffball'. When they had taken him home in such a sorry state they had decided that he needed a lot of food and milk and loving care. This he got.

He had become a great favourite with all the family. Even Terry and Kim's parents, when they got used to him, would hold him for the children whilst they got his food and milk ready and they even got used to his smell, (foxes do smell). He was just like a puppy wobbling about on his little legs getting his nose into everything. With all this loving care his coat grew fluffy and he got fatter (just like young children do). He used to chase the cat that lived next door and steal the food that was put out for the birds. Sometimes he would climb up the stairs and hide under the children's bed or steal the toilet roll when someone left it hanging long and on the ground. He really got quite mischievous.

Then one day Daddy said, 'It's time now children. Fluffball must go back to his parents – back to the wild. His mummy and daddy won't know him soon and we don't want that to happen do we?'

Terry and Kim looked sad but they understood what their daddy was saying. If wild animals have been kept by people for a long time they cannot go back to the fields or the woodlands. They are unable to find food for themselves or hide when there is danger about. The other animals won't talk to them because they have become different and more like the people. Terry and Kim knew that they would have to take Fluffball back to the woods and hoped that Ferdy and Fenella would accept him back. It would be sad for Terry and Kim but a very happy day for Fluffball.

Early in the evening Terry, Kim and Fluffball arrived in the woods. The birds were still singing, the crows and their babies were cawing, the bees were humming and the butterflies were still floating on and off the flowers that grew amongst the trees but Ferdy Fox and his wife were not anywhere to be seen.

'Oh Terry,' said Queen Kim, ' we can't leave him here all by himself.'
'We have to,' said Terry. 'Don't worry. His mummy and daddy will find him. He'll be alright.'
'Oh I do hope so. He's so small and defenceless.'
'Come on,' said Terry. 'Let's let him go now.'

They gently put Fluffball down on the ground in the soft moss that grew around the trees. Fluffball didn't look sad at all. He scuttled off into the undergrowth and ran all around the trees, sniffing and scratching at the ground.

'He's not going to miss us,' said Kim.
'No he won't miss us at all when he finds his parents,' replied Terry, 'but he'll always remember us.'

They stood and watched until Fluffball disappeared from their view and then they turned around.

'Come on,' said Terry, 'we must get home. It's getting dark now.'

Kim didn't look at Terry because she had tears running down her face but Terry knew she was crying and he put his arm around her.

'We've done the right thing,' he said. 'Babies and children belong with their mothers and fathers. It's just the same for the wild creatures.'

'I know,' said Kim, 'but I just feel so sad that we won't see him anymore.'

'We'll see him, don't you worry. If we come quietly into the woods in the early morning or the late evening, we'll see Fluffball again with all his family.' Terry wasn't sure of this but he wanted Kim to feel happier.

Kim smiled at Terry and said, 'Do you really think so?'

'I know so,' said Terry and off they walked back to the house, each with their own thoughts about Fluffball.

Fluffball was having a wonderful time. He just ran and ran and sniffed and sniffed. Then he suddenly felt a funny feeling in his tummy.

I'm hungry, he thought, where are those people that feed me? He looked around but they were nowhere to be seen. Fluffball felt worried for a moment but then he suddenly sniffed a nice smell. He thought his little nose recognised it. It smelt like him! He kept following the smell until he came to a halt in a little glade in the wood. There were trees and bushes all around him in a circle.

I must have a look in there, he thought and slowly walked over to an opening he had seen in the bushes. He sniffed round him again and found the same smell as before so he started to walk through the opening. Suddenly he heard a noise so he stopped.

What was that? he thought. Then he moved forward again to where there was more of that smell. Then a big smile crept over Fluffball's face.

'Mummy! Daddy!' he called as right in front of him stood the biggest animal he had ever seen – and it looked just like him!
'Well hello Son,' said Ferdy. 'You've come home.'
'Hello Daddy,' said Fluffball. 'Some children have been looking after me. I think their names were Terry and Kim.'
'Yes. Your mother and I know who they are,' said Ferdy. 'You were very lucky to be found by them. They've treated you very well haven't they?'
'Yes,' said Fluffball. 'They were very kind to me and I shall never forget them.'

With that Fluffball and Ferdy walked further into the hole in the undergrowth to join Fluffball's mummy and his brothers and sisters. Lucky Fluffball!

Chapter Four

Night arrived and it was warm although there was no sunshine. There were no birds singing either, just a stillness over the meadow and the woods. Harry woke up, and as usual he yawned.

I wonder if anything has happened today, he said to himself. He knew that when he met Freddy Frog he would be told all about the happenings that he had missed whilst he had been asleep. Harry didn't have any children because he was still a young hedgehog but while he was growing up he was learning all about the ways of the other animals and about Cowslip Corner and the woodland and the 'road' that the people used. The moon was shining and the bats were out flying low in the sky.

The insects must be flying low too and that means rain, thought

Harry. Well I'll be alright if it rains. It's the best weather for me if I'm out hunting. So off he started on his hunt for food. Red had gone to bed and so had Kenny. There were only the bats and Beauty to keep him company.

I'll have to go and see Beauty and see if she has any news to tell me, thought Harry. So off he trundled again through the flowers and the clover in Cowslip Corner. What a surprise he was going to have and such good news!

As Harry stopped and sniffed the air wondering when the rain was going to come one of the bats flew down very low.

When he was close to Harry he whispered 'There's been a lot of excitement in Cowslip Corner today Harry.'

Then the bat flew away leaving Harry to wonder and guess until he could find Beauty.

The rain had started to fall so it took Harry a long time to cross over the meadow towards where Beauty was sheltering under the large branches of one of the large woodland trees that hung over the meadow. Harry had found all kinds of delicious things to eat. When he had first left the hedgerow he had bumped into Freda who was scuttling home.

'Hello,' Freda said. 'I have to be careful now when I'm out and about that one of those young crows doesn't spot me. Anything they see moving in the grass they'll swoop down on. It really is quite frightening.'
Harry nodded and agreed with her and then asked politely, 'How are your children Freda?'

'Oh they're very well thank you and big enough now to find their own food. We'll be saying goodbye to each other soon although I know we'll meet from time to time in the meadow. They grow up so quickly you know.'
Harry nodded again and smiled. 'Goodbye,' he said. 'You must be on your way home to bed at this time.'
'Yes,' said Freda and as quick as a wink she was gone.

Harry trundled on stopping often to see if there was anything to eat. It was very dark now but in the distance by the river Harry thought he saw Ferdy and Fenella having a drink with their cubs. It was too dark though to see how many cubs were with them so he wasn't able to tell whether number five, (or Fluffball), was back. He looked over towards the other side of the meadow and saw the shape of Beauty in the gloom.

'Hello Beauty,' he shouted across at her.
Beauty softly neighed her 'Hello' in return. 'It's been a happy day here today,' she said.
'Has it?' asked Harry. 'Tell me what's happened.'

Beauty proceeded to tell Harry first about Blossom returning and then about Ferdy and Fenella's cub being brought back by King Terry and Queen Kim.

'That's lovely,' said Harry. 'I bet that little number 5 will be more careful now.'
'He's not so little now,' replied Beauty. 'He's the biggest of all their cubs so King Terry and Queen Kim must have fed him well. If he was still with them I'm sure he would be almost as big as me by now!'
'No,' said Harry. 'Foxes never grow as tall as horses or ponies.'

'I'm glad about that,' said Beauty, 'I don't think I'd feel very safe here if all the foxes were as big as me. I'm going back to sleep now. Take care and have a nice night.' And off Beauty walked to her favourite spot under the large tree.

Harry had all of the meadow to himself now apart from the bats who were still flying low overhead. After a long while, when Harry had eaten quite enough he decided that he would take a walk down to the river because he was thirsty. As he drew close to the river he could make out a white shape in the darkness. Whoever can that be? He thought. Whoever it is are much too large to be Davy or Dilly. He trundled on a little faster eager to know who or what the white shape was. It wasn't until he got right to the water's edge that he realised who it was.

'Susan,' he called. Susan was a beautiful white swan. She had been sleeping but she lifted her head as she heard Harry call out. 'How nice to see you again Susan,' Harry continued. 'I haven't seen you here for over half a year now. Where is your mate?'
Susan sighed and answered, 'He isn't here any longer. Some stupid people were shooting guns and they hit Sam and broke his wing. He's been taken away. Maybe one day I'll find him again because I miss him so much. I'd thought I'd swim down to Cowslip Corner and be with my friends again because I'm feeling very lonely.'
'I'm very sorry to hear that Sam has been hurt,' said Harry, 'although I'm sure everyone will be glad to see you. Kenny Kingfisher is back and Ollie and Olive Otter and Betty and Bobby Beaver are still here so you won't be lonely anymore. Oh and I nearly forgot, we've got a king and queen now. Maybe they'll

help you to find Sam but the others will tell you all about them because I have to head on home now because I'm getting very tired. It was lovely seeing you again. Bye-bye.'
'Goodbye,' said Susan and she put her head back under her wing to wait for daybreak.

Harry trundled off. He couldn't wait to get home. What a nice night it had been! It had been a nice day too! Let's hope that Terry and Kim will be able to help Susan.

THE END